MAY 17 '71

SONGS

SONGS

by Alicia Ostriker

Holt, Rinehart and Winston

New York   Chicago   San Francisco

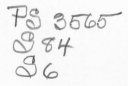

First Edition

Some of these poems were previously published in the following
periodicals: *Sewanee Review, New Mexico Quarterly, Granta,
Carleton Miscellany, Smith, Shenandoah.*
Designer: Berry Eitel
SBN: 03-081019-1 (hardbound)
SBN: 03-081248-8 (paper)
Printed in the United States of America

For the dear ones.

Edg. Men must endure
  Their going hence, even as their coming hither.
  Ripeness is all. Come on.

SONGS

The Rose Song

i

Are lovers, giving
Roses to one another,
Wary of what they tender

Do they observe
In the dark
When they unfold each other

Do they consider
Their eyes, watching
For beauty's blemish

Or how
Quickly her mouth's kiss
Dries on his skin

ii

Do they say give me that flower,
Beloved, because its thorns
Are most hurtful to me,

Because the cruelty
Of its blossom sickens me
And the smell of it shames,

And I will loathe its tedious foul
Decaying, and because it is
Not sweet nor sure

Only most faultless and most beautiful

iii

And do they say, beloved,
Our bodies, when they incline together
Are neither sweet nor sure,

But are as roses, wantonly
Shaking to every touch of wind
Or hand's touch, in their prime:

But are even as roses, performing
Obeisance to what encloses them
And will consume

Them shaking in its fell and faultless doom

The Bird Watcher

Somebody on this roof is keeping pigeons.
At seven every night he lets them go
In a great gray cloud, to circle among washlines
And silvery antennas, glinting with sunset.
One may say, a reasonable allotment of sky
For pigeons, since who ever heard of pigeons
Craving the vaulted firmament? See how they fly
Like hunched-up shoulders, denying the stretch
Of individual air. What would they do with freedom?
At a whistle, they collapse like pockets in a parachute
Back into their box on the roof.

But one, as they pass in a choked flutter
By my window, drops,
And settles in an angle of the cornice
Plumping itself like a grandma. There now—
Probably it wants bread; and if I gave,
Would stay till doomsday, filthying up my sill,
Rubbing its friendly breast against my glass,
And crooning to me its suffocating peace.
Well, it can do as it likes. I'll neither give
Nor chase it with a broomstick. I've troubles enough
Without turning God for a pigeon.

Yet there it sits. How long can it sit so
Sedately preening and staring at me there
With its fixed, tiny, stupid, glittering eyes?
It seems I have no choice, except for whether
It's fitter to be benevolent or cruel
To this my creature; there being no middle ground,
For deity, of tasteful indecision.
I only wish that someone were as willing
To play my God to me, take praise and curses
Flung from my humdrum throat—
Still there, you bird? Then take your damned crumbs! here!

A Leave-Taking

Because you will be gone, we hold the other
Still and unmeeting in the other's eyes
As pearl reflecting pearl, or shell and shell.

This day was goodly, since we did not spell
Its look aloud; rivers and lakes have skies
Only in seeing, not by touch together.

So twinly did we turn, my lover and brother,
Moving as swimmers, moved as summer's thighs
Our cloudy bodies: and the sun hung tall—

How will I keep your face? those eyes will fall
Like death upon me, pools where a serpent lies
Shaded between still reeds that never wither.

Because you do not sleep, I shall not either:
Wait, and the black will shift, and the bird cries
Swing through the window, and the morning will

Creep grayly up as soldiers. But until
The dawn comes and the sudden shadows rise,
I stay with you and watch the angels gather
Over the gravestones in your opened eyes.

After the Nervous Breakdown

I may not talk to you,
Folded boy.
I might hurt you.

Wit, pride, they have you drugged,
White, asleep.
You tried to run away this morning

To China, home
To convert the heathen
Before the hideous cross smote you.

They caught you.
So I bring you a chrysanthemum.
And I stand outside looking at you.

Some Days in March

March 13. Afternoon.

Sunlight between the blinds
Dust on the pillow
Brahms in the next room
And your hands on me
All were as if some stranger shared the bed
Smiling, and slid a cool blade in my bones.

March 14. Towards Equinox.

After many gray days, and early darkness,
Today, when I leave work, it is still bright,
And I perceive, an instant, as I am running for a bus, between
                    buildings the sun:
Great ruby, dying, dying.

March 15. Morning.

Three seconds after you left, in a brusque
Untoward fit of joy: the coffee? the kiss?
I leapt to the window, to the windowsill's level,
Dragged up the blinds and stood, to catch you, to catch *you*
Who bounded like a fox into the day.

March 16. The Grievance.

Roll out of this bed,
Go sleep in that bed.
Will you waste, for some few
Cold words of mine, one whole
And irrecoverable night, fool?

March 17. A Promise.

Time does not waste me.
If I had nothing
But wine and candles
And your touch at night, my friend,
I would survive forever.

March 18. The Thaw.

A tigerish, unnatural heat.
It makes you want to be poor
And sit on a stoop
In the evening, drinking beer, suffering.
Summer's coming.

March 19. On the Evening Bus.

That young girl with the cornstalk's soul
Is on the bus with me again.
I know her secretly,
How under the awkward (trying to look like the other girls)
Flimflam, she is pale green,
Veined, and with strength.
How she might (will not) might swallow the sun in her beauty
Were she once undressed, with her face washed very clean.

March 20. Frost Again.

The trees are climbing
Over the hill.
The vines are climbing
Over the trees.
They do not breathe.

March 21. Equinox.

All day I could sleep
Until white spiders came
And spun threads between
Finger and finger
And dust settled on my hair
And Spring went away weeping.

9

On the Perfectibility of Mankind

So I turned into a sty
And laid me down among the swine.

                    —*William Blake*

Now that the truth is out in black and white,
Now that the Cause of Causes is made clear,
And any common thief can answer right
The analyst his well-appointed stare,
And every pebbly schoolboy can recite
The canons of his popular despair—

God being dead (I killed him said cock robin;
No I did said the sparrow; no I did:
Me said the flea. His end was passing tragic.
I pricked him with my little pointed logic—)
God being dead, I say, how does it come
The Devil flourishes so healthily
And that we nourish him and feed ourselves
On what we feed, so game, so filthily?

In College Town, Autumn

Before ever the silver cord be loosed,
or the golden bowl be broken, or the
pitcher be broken at the fountain, or
the wheel broken at the cistern.

—Eccl. 12.6.

All the gay glad girls, the young men
Happy as horses in heavens of hay,
With bosoms bouncing and blouses bare
With rinse and streak in the sunny smelling hair
With trousers tight over thighs, as fair
They trot in the street, no shame to spare,
Rub one another and trot again
Strut in the noon in the streaming day.

Year after year, young they appear
As grass grows green, to the aged eye.
But the aged head says they will fade
As fowl freeze when the white frost falls
And suddenly south they fly, or would lie dead,
And a few leaves drop on the tops of garden walls;
But the young fly steadfast north, nor ever fear
That the aged, eyeing them, sigh.

We see the faithful fountain rise
From summer towns up to the skies,
Silver and white are in our eyes;
We never see the hand that moves
To the due switch, or the valve's grooves,
And the fountain falls, to our surprise
Like the drooping bone of a man who dies
Sated upon his lady's thighs
And sleeps, and not this night will prize
Again those breasts of hers that are like doves.

The Going Hence, the Coming Hither

Agony, shock: which is my birth, my death,
My clumsy woman's body being torn,
How is it, could I tell you, born, unborn,
Your knitted seed was made articulate?

Your flesh is not my flesh, not for my cares,
Nor bone my bone in gratitude for pain.
Back into counted time is all my gain:
Close windows   open chimneys   empty doors—

Behold my future joy, a newmade thing
Unfolded in the house: song without words
His mouth tastes lilac, out of his hands grow birds,
He sings, and there is no finish to his singing.

Goes out stained white; the sun is halfway over
Orchards away, throbbing as if it bled,
Some six winds kiss, the boy leans down his head
To hear perhaps deep thunder in the clover.

Then turning round he backs against a tree
Whose branches open apples over him,
Then perhaps voices out of blossoms come
And wind him head to foot in ecstasy—

Comes back stained green. Trust, I will not disturb
What is not mine. He keeps his tipping dream,
Seeing I know such equilibrium
As his, one least touch tumbles; hence this curb

On my own hands restrains them from the deep
Apple-filled baskets of his helpless sleep.

Three for Music

1. Black, Black

Black, black smoke stacks
Line the gray industrial sky.
The East and Hudson Rivers meet,
Ships of the world go flowing by.
I am heavy, I am blind.
Ease for me my grievous wound.

Poison melts the ear to flame,
Sickness rots the heart to song.
All my brothers in the war,
All my fathers beaten, wrong.
I am heavy, I am blind.
Ease for me my grievous wound.

Come from forests of your sorrow,
Skin be shining like the sun.
Walk a road between the poplars,
Rest where diamond rivers run.
Burn in the star as the star burns down.
Ease for me my grievous wound.

Do not think, when I embrace you,
Arm will shrink and tongue run dry.
Do not think, now if I face you,
Under the flesh white bone must lie.
Burn in the star as the star burns down.
Ease for me my grievous wound.

Now take off your words and clothing,
Now stand barefoot on my soil.
Let the streams meander singing,
Blood mix with honey, milk mix with oil.
Mouth of the poppy can make no sound.
Ease for me my grievous wound.

2. Fine Woven Rain

And lightning splits the sky
Thunderclouds hide the sun.
Fine woven rain comes down,
Fine woven rain.

All summer long brings fruit,
Each morning brings the lark.
Your solitary people
Grow on into the dark.

A pilot flies on courage,
Hand and brain and skill,
He aims his eggs to drop
Down for the highest kill.

Down in the long rye grass
Lie a young girl and boy.
They are not sure of misery
And they have no words for joy.

A woman late at night
Is rocking her wakened child,
Giving it milk to suck
And keeping it from the cold.

At midnight the tired astronomer
Is dreaming that he spells
From numbers something perfect,
As the stars pursue their wheels,

And the spirit builds his walls,
The separate lives grow full.
Who shall comfort their despair?
Who shall make them whole?

And lightning splits the sky
Thunderclouds hide the moon.
Fine woven rain comes down,
Fine woven rain.

3. Ribbon

The brighter a ribbon, the quicker it slips.
I had no man but one.
Green grass is growing on his lips
So all his singing is done.

Though he be brown as a berry bark
And stubborn to hold as a river,
If once I touched him the silver dark
Would twine the gift to giver.

So sweet the thrush whistles, so easy it dies,
But I never knew to wrong him.
He'd sleep with weeds behind his eyes
And my light love along him.

Girl's Song

I went out in the world afraid.
All the other people were dancing.
The sun glared, and I did not know
My face, or my hands, or whom to turn to.

I wish the sky would move as I move.
Mother, it is not you I love.

Amy Thirteen

We have a little sister and she hath no breasts.
What shall we do for our sister in the day when she shall
be spoken for? If she be a wall, we will build upon her a
battlement of silver. But if she be a door, we will enclose
her with boards of cedar.

i

Sister, we love each other
From afar, like birds:
You a little skittish sparrow
And I an ostrich, or a pedant penguin,

I bring you book-talk
Like laying fish at your feet
Meaning all that while
To say don't fear me, child.

Language useless between us: I always ask
How you are doing at school: error,
Dearest, for you always want
To talk about horses, swimming, archery, ping-pong.

I touch in my mind the fringe on your moist forehead
And your thin legs and your long rainy hands;
I watch your throat tighten when someone lies
And how you shudder and veer from big people's touch,

You so proud to refuse the kisses of the silly—
And I explode like fireworks when I remember
Going to bed you have come in your pajamas
Of your own accord and kissed my face goodnight.

Once we went swimming together,
Sister, I watched you change, I peered at you
And saw your small leaf breasts and woman's hair
So suddenly begun, like summer thunder:

Let her alone.
And I thought, go well, fly bird, fly.

ii

For you, mother, all day dying
Burdened by what implacable old fear
Blinded by what bright glass splinter long ago
Where the dust is multiplying in your corners
Where even your guppies thrive on garbage
And even your fierce window pot plants
Choke out the light
But you, you alone, dwarf mama, you do not grow:
How if I lay you, meek mother, down in my lap
And stroked your wrinkling face and soothed your dry breasts
Or opened your fingers one by one kissing your palms,
Would that bewildered face
Then pucker babylike and collapse and drop away like powder?
Would there appear behind it the girl's face with beautiful eyes?

For you, father, who no longer laugh
(Yes, I remember it, yes in my memory you
A young man, upright, my lovely young father
Playful about me, fountains of love inspiring
The dark curls looped over your eyes, and your crooked grin
But what has become of you, who has stolen you)
Shall I dance naked before you again?
Shall I cavort? Shall I do somersaults?
Shall I show you all my tricks? Shall I sing you my own
                    invented songs?
Would you then deeply draw your breath?
Would you chuckle at your clever monkey
And hoist me up on your shoulders, parade me about?
Oh you would run away shameful and crying fear.

iii

They are lost, they are lost
My father and my mother
I cannot save you
You'll never return.
My mother and my father
I will live twice for you
If you are dead
I will be living still
I will haul up
More life from my blood
I will fling forth
More songs in your silence,
I will unfurl
More joys at the sun
More furies at the stars
More flowers at the abyss,
Only for love of you,
Spent in your name.

iv

What shall we do for our sister in the day.
Shield her, save her, keep her from calamity
When the storms arrive, when the greedy world snatches.
Ribbon her round, she is frail, she is ours. . . .
Angels desire her. Let their great rushing wings
Cover her over with secret silver.

What shall we do for our sister in the day.
Let her rise up like a tree putting forth blossoms.
Golden is the air, ruby is the day.
Let her unbraid her tangled hair.
Let sparrows nestle weeping in her bosom
And robins leap on her hands.

This Room. Your Absence.

i

The room is lit.
It is the place where I am.
I am   God   damn
It

Caught
Crawling alive inside a bulb head.
I am sewn in the bed
I have bought.

Here's husbanded flesh
That will not yield to any lover.
I dash
Against you like a sea. I wish it were over.

ii

Undulations
Among the springtime boughs.
Soft brooks, midnight hands.

Desire grows, grinds, tosses.

Bravery

In Mem. ME, JFK, MX, AS, MLK, RFK . . .

Good Teacher, that rat
Was not in you, said you. I thought
Upon the plop, plop of its body, its hairless tail.
Decay it devours. It jumps fast, a bullet.

But you were buying the drinks, the Chinese
Waiter knew you, you had been so
Kindly reading my songs, your pacific face
Was a sad flag. I believed you.

We are cloistered here. I wished you, under merciless
Spots, after forty-eight wild
Interrogatory hours in the cellar, to confess.
After all, in anger I smack my child

And enjoy it. Papa, you *never?* Hardly ever? This morning
More beauty is dead in hopeless hospital.
Ah, hyacinth. Rome, Rome, over again.
The television will do the funeral

Very well, tastefully,
Assassinations are the newest industry
In this country. In this country the shit
Is about up to our knees, and there are crisp

Green bills in the pocket of the tunneling rat
Who loves those fumes. Don't tell me
You were crying, Mack.
I have my songs, that bravery.

For Barbarians: A Thesiad and Sequel

1. The Prodigy

When the other toddlers upset his sand piles
He flew in a rage. He built. Cylinders, cones,
Cubes, he lived with. His tutors suffered; if
They tried to tell him boys' tales about

Ghosts and giants—if they even mentioned
His grandfather the famous trumpeter—
He said they smelled, to wash. It was chaos. What
Can you do with a kid like that? He built

Elaborate towns like nothing in the world.
They watched him working out before he built.
The thing to do with beasts was hunt them down,
The thing to do with men was make them dwell

By alabaster, where the gods would be
Pillared erect. He said he saw men dancing.

2. Prolegomenon

As in the *Minotauromachy,* where
Soft guts gush from a central horse which bears
A semi-naked lady, who, dying,
Regards the monster that has ravished her
Yet points her lateral sword away from him
While Christ escapes, and eyes watch, from a gray house:

Most visceral cosmopolis, framed of baked dung
And steel, whose noise is death and deep
Voluptuousness to strangers, may you body forth
Some poised Ariadne, candle and thread in hand,
Some absurd child, sober, unwitting priestess
Chastely to guard your venomed labyrinths—
Your suck of city to a country boy—
And guide the hero come to enter you.

3. This Dreamer Cometh

She was grinning like a whore—she had big teeth—drinking
And lying there, plastered with baubles to her knees,
And toenails painted. Then these little girls
Pranced in singing some of their foreign songs.

To oil me, she said. God! me to lie down like a skinned
Codfish in that room, surrounded by mirrors,
And everybody looking. They all do. You cannot
Tell the men from the eunuchs: so musical, so refined.

I tell you, it disgusted me to think
Of the thousands rotting in their mines, the young boys in
                          their fleets
Broken, scurvied, for the sake of that rich bitch
Making small talk, for the sake of some spit on a wave.

History will change that. You know about her,
I gave her what she asked, and sailed home here.

4. The Eagle

He has forgotten how he mounted here. His immense
Vans winnow the air. His heart really works;
It was wound up once, and squeezes like muscle.
The filaments flash off, on, off, on, someone
Wants something. Down there it is warm.

It is an atmosphere of moist
Dependencies sticking together, the green and pink
Divisions gently warming and eating each other.
Those signalers, they spot the map like measles;
Earth sweats them, and they want things. It would be easy

Labor now, tacking upward toward the poisonous
Fiery mirror and shattering radiation
Of the near-vacuum; but the Law says he must
Plummet upon that world of ants, for love.

5. The Coal Freighter

Out on a passive sea all day we steam
Forward. With flag and black stones. Our engineer
Despises the captain, our mate has discipline
Problems, our cook is bored with endless sheer
Sunlight and alien ports, feels cheated of romance, and gossips.

Nevertheless, all noon the golden boys
Up in the air are painting the masts against rust;
And in the evening apprentices making no noise
Gather each other's motions as they practice
Morse code across the dark bridge, by the light
Of cigarette tips; and the young ensign with a fool's face
Alone at dawn on watch fingers a flute

As the sky whitens, as our wake shows fair,
As beyond this sea our enemies prepare.

The Astronomer's Mate

Wives of great men all remind us
We can make our lives sublime
And, departing, leave behind us
Sootprints on the hands of Time.

You lie in your obnoxious undershirt
Thinking about the job
You have to unpeel far suns
And become famous.
It is after dinner, you are about to fall asleep
But I do not hit you with a block,
Head of equations, cosmos problem dreamer,
I speak sweetly. It is not what the movies and novels
Led me to expect. It is all effort,
All uphill, always hopeless. We are true.
Tongue, pump, hand, eye.

So have another beer, honey.
The ticker's thudding hard, and the harder
It labors, the quicker clots. Those big red stars
Called giants thunder a mere hundred million
Years of perpetual core explosion
Using up hydrogen. When the heat's off,
A body dies. A body's beauty dies.
Pressure and energy to bulge them, like
The stupid wars we need to keep us up,
Brandishing rods of knowledge, painted bowls,
To rule, to catch, the spiral stellar tails,
The spill of dragon's breath, they finish.

Let us suppose these conflagrations wish
To burn forever. As we have told the doctor,
Our family histories are heart troubled.
That kills our people off, if they are lucky;
Worse jests, if not. Be famous, love. Live long.
Perform. Up we go, then, upstairs, to bed,
To fight again another day.

Lord, lord, it's time to pray.
Entropic One, freezer of galaxies,
King of White Dwarfs, unscrupulous Absence, hear me.
You see this spectacled wonder and myself?
May we become a toddling old couple.
May we make quaint appearance at weddings and funerals.
May we be a curiosity
Until wood splinters in the bowels of dragons,
Until the pitcher shivers at the well-curb,
Until the pump clogs. Understand me now.
Let neither of us tend the other's cancer,
But race for whose heart stops first, his or mine.

Elegy

December 20, 1965

What may I tell? The sharp death that does not leave
nor rich men nor high: it him took.

—*Saxon Chronicle*

i

In Doom Year, the day of his number,
My sole striding father was humbled.
His heart hurt a moment, he fell vacated,
And hit that sidewalk, if there is mercy, dead.

ii

These are my visions: knife vision driving
Alone towards you the given stiffclothed bittercold man
Around whom vertical overcoats gaze
Horrified, gluttonous, breathing—
And vision in the hospital basement
While the dirty balding coroner jokes,
You and I meet, who never meet again,
Although I establish unalterably glassed
Hard forehead's breadth from temple to temple,
Sleeping eyes, left tightened cheek bruised brown,
Ironic mouth that speechlessly bids me
Stay with you, be eternal.
And vision of the burning
While we prayed to the spider God
And screamed behind our eyelids,
The boxed brainpot, depository
Of school verse and love's future gesture
Takes fire, steams, the diffident tongue is eaten,
The racing leg collapses,
The tender life of testicles withers,

Now the marrowbones lose their juice,
Now the teeth and vertebrae drop
Glowing, incandescent among cinders,
At last the stubborn clotted heart is punished,
While we sleepwalk from the chapel to the car
Quiet now, quiet now
Quiet now he is burning no more.

iii

Must not the widow pass strange hours,
Having lain beside one man forever,
Having his odors still in the house,
Having us love one another because we grieve?

iv

Curse this. All our lives swear hatred
Of the abominable enemy, that
Is the condition of our breath, and yet
Now no rage rises, why, no anger,
No outburst, why, but we are anchored
To quietude, as if a stranger
From the deep night entered a room
Blinking shyly at our bright lights,
Who, before anyone spoke to him,
Returned alone into his snowy night
As in tales the wild bird goes, takes flight.

Cassandra: Variations

1. The Initiate

I was no beauty, even as a child.
But gazing on the daughter of a king, they all said
"Loveliest of daughters," and would have married me
By flattering the gullible ancient, my father.

He would have chosen some bulge-muscled lout,
They all supposing I, a mere girl, conceived
Nothing of this. That was in the old time
When we counted cows and I lived with my sisters,

Before our familiar troubles. So I went then
And bribed the priestesses to let me burn
Upon your painted altars thighs of lambs
Wrapped in thick fat of strong and pleasing savour.

Also I worshipped down in our barley meadows.
Alone I lay, shy, having first rubbed
My body with crushed oils of ochreous flowers,
Letting the pollen lie stuck to my skin:

Slow, I became again calm beast, rich plant
Solemnly sweating under noon heat, unstirring;
Bright tinted insects buzzed above my eyes,
I waited, fasted, prayed, desiring you.

You came. And now no man of them will have me.
I walk in the streets raving at every pebble.
Scions of gentlemen throw clods at me
Because I, seeing, have cursed them playing soldiers.

My father wishes I were never born.
"Seditious bitch," my gleaming brothers say.
Am I not fearsome, being thus consecrate?
You, Lord of Light, I hate you with my soul.

2. The Vow

Let there be no fresh evil done.

Bear you a son! My lord, I believe you intend
No malice, but this coin of evil you
Have not, nor we, willing desired to spend,

Once minted, merely circulates, falls like dew.
Thus creature murders creature without end
And the gods repose, as having nothing to do;

Helpless as we? Perhaps, my shining friend.
Howbeit, this my flesh shall make no new
Flesh for the manglers in their mirth to rend.

3. The Mantis

The last I saw, a lizard ran from the sun.
Then not I, but this other woman
Screamed again, falling
Once again screamed falling into her sea
Of pain, she fought back furious against my

Outrage, shame to flesh and to earth shame
And the light descended and the light came
Calmly sailing.

Then as the slender fluke dragged out ashore
In nets from her cool waters thrashes air,
And cries untongued, O Prince! to the fisherman, Not
Your air for me, it is too thin, too bright
To bear; or as throughout the starry night
In vacant fields a rabbit gnaws the foot
The iron traps, to its bone, but when the morning
Comes with the plowman, shrieks before his shining
Knife splits her skin: so that voice cried
Not see, not see, let me not see
This, it is not for me
It is too bright—then flashing fell the blade.

Woke, the brain bleeding, I bride
Cast forth again, and again, how slowly mind
Contracts, cracking while cooling, like stretched metal.
Now there is but the ordinary stench
Of death about me in this sacred town.
About me rise the little cries of children
And in each house heroes' wives braid and bind
Their hair, and someone is whipping a slave, and
Afar, far off, the hunting gods halloo.

4. The Single Combat

Our correspondent informs us the Assembly
Of the Royal Family has, after lengthy and serious
Deliberation, voted unanimous
Assent to the recent controversial offer
Of our Crown Prince on behalf of our liberty
And honor. Listeners, a historic decision
Has been made here, we all realize. Following the vote,
The Family and its closest advisers held
A gala feast, in which two hundred spotless
Sheep were consumed. A corps of Dexter Sons
Regaled the Prince with thrilling demonstrations
Of troop maneuvers and war yells. The Chorus of Bastards
Next rendered in eight-part fugue a new Toast to our Lady
Of Argos, and the daughters, in flowered robes
Of Java silk, performed libations and danced.
The new Assembly Hall, as you know, designed by a team
Of Thracian architects, has a gold floor
For feasts and sacrifices, which doubles as a dance floor.
I am told now that a brief uproar threatened
To disturb the festivities, when a girl, said to be
One of the daughters, stood up and began shouting
Pacifist slogans. She was escorted out quietly
And no names named. It seems this young woman has long been
Suspected of collusion, although until this time
Official Palace word has claimed she suffers
Under a medical disability. We are expecting
A special interview with the Family doctor
Within the hour. The girl is believed to have

No following here, and plans for the combat continue,
Scheduled for noon, and a fine day for it.
  My listeners will be glad to hear the Prince
Is confident of immediate victory,
And all of us will join with him in hoping
For a speedy end to this terrible conflict, when
The foe will be driven out, and the just cause triumph, bringing
Peace to our children and our children's children.

5. The Funeral | *look upon him*
                if ever you were joyful when
                    you saw him come back
                living from battle: for he was a great joy

Now sounds the song of lamentation loud.
Now multitudinous throats of his women boom
From rafter to rafter of this well-wrought palace,
Moaning from heavy bowels the unendurable woe.
Son of a king, city-protector, slaughterer of men, we grieve.

Fire for the human form I loved. In the morning
We shall gather his white bones and wrap them in purple
Robes for the hollow grave. The women will need heart's ease
And invent tricks of a god to explain his cowardice.
Son of a king, city-protector, slaughterer of men, we grieve.

I should have been this shameless lovely whore.
None would perceive in my ivory face the tracks
Of my filth's feet. I'd languish with deep grace.
Souls of huge men would weep to behold the distress of my weeping.
Son of a king, city-protector, slaughterer of men, we grieve.

I should have been a sponge, my honest sister,
Oscula swaying to one good man's life;
Filled up, and now squeezed out, go into exile,
Find a man fair again, fill up, accommodate.
Son of a king, city-protector, slaughterer of men, we grieve.

I should have been sag-glanded Hecuba
With half a hundred sons out of my belly
Spawned like fish-seed: what luxury, when each
Died, to let oily tears drip slowly down my jowls.
Son of a king, city-protector, slaughterer of men, we grieve.

Slave girls attending, tell me, if the body
Captured, trots tame and common, might the mind
Go mad, wither at last, and leave one free?
Corpses of brave young men, tell me, how tastes the knife?
Son of a king, city-protector, slaughterer of men, we grieve.

The Anniversary

Of course we failed, by succeeding.
The fiery cherub becomes his smothering,
A greedy heart dives into a dream
Of power or truth, and wakes up middle-aged
In some committee room.
It is eating paper instead of God.
We two are one, my bird, this is a wedding.

When love was war, you swore you'd burn
Your life and die at thirty-five. I said good riddance,
Bright hairy boy, I will beat you, down,
Tear you to monkey shreds, survive like earth,
Owl-eyed, because I wanted to see everything
Black and permanent and kill you with your theories.
We used to wake up sweaty and entangled.

Thirty, home, and work. We cohabit in a functioning machine.
There is violence, somewhere else. Do we wish this? It occurs,
The flayed combatant, the dismembered child,
The instruments in the basement. We must wish it. See,
Between us is peace, our babies are plump,
I know you, I caress you, I fail you. My faith adheres
In nothing. Don't leave me, don't leave me.

The Hunt

i

   Skull in the bed
I saw a gray person never before

   Skull in the bed
Skin wrinkled asweat trembling

That was a bear's big flesh and commandeering chest
Dropped tubed nose veins bladder leather strapped could not breathe

By himself frightened of the tubes in his nose
Could not breathe chest up and down toes stiff

   Skull in the bed that last week lorded
The passover festival my father in the wilderness

   Skull in the bed
Afraid of colored nurses

   Skull in the bed my jacket
My tie right his hospital coarse death pajamas flopping

   Skull in the bed
Tore the tubes out of his nose

The nurse ran away roaches danced on the walls mother
I held my father all night in my arms

ii

Oh you bastards oh you damned bastards
Get your hands off me get your hands off me you
Signed it legal my lawyers you meddle with me
Vermin cowboys you won't need a lawyer you'll need
A doctor yes a coroner think I don't smell it
Disgusting troubles for everybody a busted
Pipe more like sewer I catch stealing the injustice
Oh swindlers and scum the stink and the elevators
Broken again barbarians hide
And get you at night the odor a knife
In my back with a blade in the groin but I yell
They are dragons they burn us with orders with writhing
And stop running and stop twisting and a pogrom and that bulb
Trying to kill me they are trying to kill me trying to kill me

iii

Number One Operation "inconclusive." Waiting now
In the new room, in the windows of morning
Wheet-wheet, wheeoo, wheeoo. Green spurts the grass
And green the great Park elms. The dewy strollers
Breathe deep and let their collies loose to run
Among the mist. And all day long it shines:
Maids from Park Avenue chatter on benches, their uniforms
Are blue-white under the sun, themselves full of scandal,
Their baby-carriage wheels squeak, the infants gurgle, being
                    rocked,
Toddlers discover stones, discover robins, a boy snatches a

Car from a fat girl; both howl; the maids whip over indignantly.
Boys play ball. Thud, go the baseballs in mitts. Lovers
Lie hip to hip in the grass and kiss, their lips
Sweat, their portables pour fruit of sound
Over their eyes, the fruit falls thumping and rolling
About on the sweet earth, transforming, melting.
A bald clerk feeds pigeons calling cluck cluck come here, come
                    here, come here,
Black lads strut, old men absorb heat and are silent,
The skin of their chests, lily-white with sparse black hairs,
Shows through transparent and slippery nylon shirts,
Traffic hoots down along Fifth Avenue, mingling
Chrysalid sounds, sweet sounds, that rise like twisting candle
                    smoke
Into the distinct blue air of summer, hang pleasantly brightly
Outside his window and dance. And waiting now
(Roses, roses all the way) my mother
Says we are grateful he remains with us
And goes home hysterical. As for myself,
I can do nothing useful. Mother, try to eat.
"They lie, for their reputations. They must keep safe."
Mother, try to sleep. Mother, wear a new dress.
"Oh how did it happen, tell me. Oh how did it happen."
Between handkerchiefs, nevertheless, she turns executive.
Stealing good nurses from other patients, she cries:
"Miss X, you are so good with him, Miss Y, you know how to
                    handle him,
(None of these bitches will work without bribes.
They are always having coffee, they are always somewhere
                    else. What
About when his wound opened? My God, blood all over . . .)
Miss Z, you are such a comfort to me." Waiting,
Behold, after work, the clan of prosperity,
Causing my wonder, what doth it profit a man,
Patriarch, to inspire these paunchy loyalties,
Gathering shuffle-footed, making hearty and comfortable noises,
Female and male, the enormous family, the uncle
I hit on the head with a hammer once, the poker cronies
With embarrassed shoulders, the eager young partners from
                    downtown

Daily like bulls, that bump like unhappy but
Gaudy balloons through Reception up along
The septic corridor a grisly green
From door to door into this room, this confinement.
They excite him, he laughs, bullies, whines, weakens, coughs,
                    his hands
Wobble on the white sheets, they do not remove
Themselves, he hurls and struggles, shaggy one—
          A trail of roses fouls the corridor
Waiting for Number Two, waiting for more.

iv

This lot of faces, what are they bothering for?
Dummies, who needs them? If they wouldn't do everything wrong,
With meals and shots and this business of turning me over
And carrying me to the bathroom and back from the bathroom,
Which I could do without, and dressing and undressing
This thing in my side, or if maybe the boils went away,
If maybe the supposedly necessary blood drops
Dripping in the arm from your poor imitation
Of a bottle of sparkling burgundy bubbling hitched
To the bed would stop splashing the walls, it's bad
For the paint job, so much blood; if those ladies—
I always liked a hefty woman, but
These are tremendous, and still after me
With medieval tortures, with plagues,
Caterpillars in the soup, no I'm fooling—
Along with their mustache medics stayed home, if maybe
The pain would stop a minute, life would be beautiful.
A little smile, a little push, I always say.
Intelligence. You got to have it here.

v

Am I simply expected to be near
You, staying at evening, when you fall,
Deliberately as a rotten cedar
Inclines, then crashes, among cool immobile
Forests, into your vacuous and moaning terror

39

While mom takes dinner and we both hope
She will return speedily, against our panic
And my repulsion? Father, what shall I say?

       Wait for me. Let me tell you. You are deluded.

Am I expected, on the contrary,
To be trapped into words, words, to become a fountain
Of wisdom, a rock of certitude, a pillar
Of faith, a joy dove, a stream of assurances
Sprung from the living platitude to water
The thirsty fortitude, little David harping
And happy for mad Saul? Too hard, too hard, don't
Try anything. I will bring magazines.

       Wait for me. Let me tell you. You are deluded.

Here I come, father, bearing roses.

vi

The principle is like poker, to cut your losses
And let your profits run. In life, in life.
Buy cheap sell dear. What will the market do?
The market will fluctuate. Suffer fools to get
Out at the bottom for you. Heart, it is only
For the dear ones. When they cannot take care
Of themselves, you walk in. Provide.

       And all this while the velvety melon feeding

They are wonderful sons. Raise them to be gentle.
Wisdom, flower of the tongue, my seed.
Mathematics, the violin, spare nothing. Let them
Be at my feet. Speak to each other.
Speak of the world, speak of the times coming.
Indians starve. Neglect no opportunity.
In the Old Country, you would be soap now.

       And all this while the velvety melon feeding

Listen. On Fridays there is wine,
Candles and prayers. That is how
It should be now. Before, was the poolhall,
The track. Good. It is a question
Of a sense of balance. Listen. We used to go
Fishing in New Jersey. And after dark
The Italians would sing.

vii

Some day a long
Time from now I hope we shall be
Rocking on a trellised
Porch with morning glories
In the middle of summer.
That house shall have clean
Linen and good liquor.
I will explain to you
The elegance of quantum
Mechanics. Snowflakes
Falling, we shall be
In a warm living room
High over the city.
I will tell you
How John Keats,
That sensuous man, grew
To fill his life, as an apple
Fills its peel. When roses
In June unfold their red graves,
Touching your sleeve, I will outline
The decline of Rome. My eloquence
You will comprehend. Leaves
Falling shall find us
Up in the mountains
Beside a wild lake.
I shall demonstrate
From the concatenation
Of ripples of several stones,
The music of Bach,
Blue link to link.

viii

Oh then in the morning we bombed along back
Passing the bottle, the stars hanging down,
The summer moon, the pig farms passing,
The road opening, the wind for sobriety,
Oh you were king, man, you were king
And you drove the bridge like a maniac's dream.

ix

I shall say your crime
Makes the stomach turn,
Unctuous Sir. A filthy
Way to be. I shall say
To my father, since
I have sought you within
The gates and beyond
The gates, forever, more
Than a woman, more
Than a child, beloved,
And I follow you, you are
My fate, what is falsehood
Within betrays us. I shall
Say behold the man, a shell
With eyes becoming hot
Yellow, darting foxily, not
My father any more,
Nobody, nobody can bear
To think what poison
Swims his flesh and thin
World, what gluttonous
Sponge sucks up his
Blood, enthroned on some dank
Dunghill in his body as
The captive creatures, heart,
Liver, lungs, strung nerves,
Bow down under its scourge
And his wound pulses

42

With its energy, it grows
In him as I grew
In my mother, putting
Forth now a foot, now
A fat finger, taking
Foetal time. I shall at last
Say stand you beast
Dear God my friend because
Behold him now my father
My father and from this
Nettle and from this nettle
My lord fool, what flower
King cancer, festering weeds—

x

And all this while I have been playing with beads.
My mama gave me them. Did she, little girl.
(For the daughters, a poor thing, chain of chill lustrous
                        glass beads
About the neck, clustered in the hand, fingered, pressed to the
                        eyes, to the mouth, licked, nibbled)
Girl, you are teasing me, girl, you are shivering,
Girl, you are lovely, lie with me, my warm.

xi

Father, the murder dream
In which I slew the bear
Was false, yet among the black pines
It seemed most vivid blood.
And the beast becomes a bush
Of roses unconsumed
In the fires from heaven to heaven
Which bless me. I will be good,
No fear, fear no more.

xii

Wrap him up in tissue paper
Send him down the 'cinerator
One, two . . .
　　　Come home, come home
Up the hill, up the stairs, into the house, it's time.

xiii

From Westchester, smart slash-mouth daughters, converge! From uptown & downtown, nervous brothers, converge! From Harlem, dark women with harp voices, smooth immaculate-hosed women, women of large white shoes and delicate caps, converge! From twilit knee-deep carpeted surgeons' offices, Swedish the lounges, Japanese the ashtrays, hawkboned impassioned falterless mental hands, hissing cold spotlight rays from expensive eyes, converge!

From labeled bloodvats in the basement waiting pint by pint nodding & sparkling, you little life drops, converge! From a stripped mountain making the ugly cities & the Pennsylvania firemills, you fine steel, you disinterested flickering accurate instruments, converge! From months of tumid jungle sun or from grubby laboratory, you mysterious chemicals, converge! From a happy rubber tree, you sterile gloves, converge! help him now! be bold!

Yellow and golden, yellow and golden
The light from the window, the light from the door,
The stripes on the table, the stripes on the floor,
Raisins will go in it, apples will go in it,
Cinnamon will go in it, sugar will go in it,
See the flat dough roll, thinner than wings.
The fat garbage man will get you.
Hey, the fat garbage man will get you.
Hey, he will put you in his bag.
Hey, he will put you in his little pot. He will cut you up into
mushrooms.
Better watch out, he will eat you. Stop crying. Stop crying.
Mama, I don't want to go there. I don't want to go there.
Mamaleh, children hit me. I don't want to go there.
The black garbage man will get you.
Kid, the black garbage man will get you.
Kid, he will take you into his black house.
Kid, he will take you down into his cellar.
He will put you on the wet floor with the roaches.
He will carry you there and he will put you in the furnace with
the garbage,
If you don't stop crying.
I don't want to go there. Mama, I burned my finger. I hurt
my foot.
Mama, my belly hurts. I want my little mother, I want my little
papa.
Shut up. Little papa is dead.
No! No! No! No!

A vase of roses glistens in the window.

In the Mountains

In the mountains
The stream falls down
Where I would be always.

My heart rains
Down too, sometimes, when my children
Strike it like lightning.

My heart turns
Over and floods still
When you, old

One, old beloved
Moving with one
Motion that is beautiful,

Create a rift in nature that cracks the stone
Open, and makes it run.
But in the mountains

Where no man lives
It is very hot, it is very cold
Always. The trail goes upward,

Rocks surmount each other,
Thin air makes fever
For the climber

Who reaches water
Lucidly riding over stone. Sounds fill
His ears, the stream falls down, he has his will.

Unser Kampf: Poems in War Time

1. One More Mouth | *We are told that on the arrival of the news of the unfortunate battle of Fontenoy, every heart beat, and every eye was in tears. But we know that no man ate his dinner the worse.*

—Samuel Johnson

Let one more sincere
Mouth talk the horror of the war
To me. I'll tell it off:
Turn dust, turn marble! Grief
Immobilizes; but you make poems
About it, and at night
You curl around the wife's
Warm haunches like anybody
Who is not crazy
And I make a poem about
You making a poem
About it, and about how bravely we,
Friend, marching give flowers away
For sweet peace and love, flowers
Soft as the faces of bankers,
And how we read in the papers
Words that would make us vomit
Our coffee, if we
Lived in that country
Or hurt more than the man
Who uses the telephone
To make bombs drop like rot
On innocent and guilty
Who then go up in fire

Or get pellets screwed in their backs
Or cannot have their rice
Because it has been poisoned.
Even a life full of choice
Proceeds imprisoned.
We should desire
A holy fire
To focus, to scorch out the eyes.

2. Vox Populi

The people, yes, are the poets. Let me make that clear.
A soldier's talk being, you see,
Brisker than yours or mine, naturally
Brings matters, as it were, to a head:
"Kilroy was here"
With his curious nose looking flip
All over Europe;
Or what the G.I. said
To the *Times* man in the Asian jungle,
Employing the Nickname Game
Of primitive art, whereby *Viet Cong*
Is *Victor Charlie,* or politely *Charles,*
To wit a symbol, because those
Yellow folk inside the flame
May as easily be grandmothers or infant girls,
Not male at all—with sensuous imagery
For a true, direct, and vivid statement:
"I love the smell of Charlie burning."
We see how clear a thing
Language becomes here, and are perforce content;
The line is poetry. Poets, remember this.
"I love it," he added for rhetorical emphasis.

3. The Wrestling: Let Be, Sustain |

Ein Gott vermags. Wie aber, sag mir, soll
Ein Mann ihm folgen durch die schmale Leier?

—*Rilke*

You have been talking about murder
In some wish to contain some furor;
It is a part. And meanwhile
Children are bursting like flowers,
Flowers are ringing like children, sun and moon
Riding like lovers, many long
Lovers, charioteers, over a hard
Earth, mountains, hard ocean
Flown would be trumpeting—
All, all we have not sung or shown,
That live and die on beauty's horn,
They wither when we do not see.
They blacken if we will not be
Bright images.

The beech trees hold the weather.
They stand for us outside
Our window, looking
At their branches, like heaven
Or this world, with their
Pleasant leaves shaking,
Their soaked trunks in the rain,
Their bending boughs in a gust.
All day they make a space. All night
They journey for our sakes.
When we wake, in our bed, in our box,
There they are, carrying the primrose
Dawn down, because their arms
Are so white, are so stout. We must
Grow stronger, love,
Speak, inexhaustibly.

Alicia Ostriker is thirty-one years old, Associate Professor of English at Rutgers University, New Jersey, and the mother of two daughters. In 1965, the University of Wisconsin Press published her non-fiction book, VISION AND VERSE IN WILLIAM BLAKE.

DATE DUE